From Generation to Generation

A Story of Nigeria from Father to Son

By

*Oladosu Awoyemi, co-written by Tobi &
Femi Awoyemi*

For permission requests, please email the publisher at Hello@ EarnestPublishers.com

ISBN – 978-1-80068-846-9

Printed in the United Kingdom. Independently Published.

Foreword

I have been searching for kid-friendly Yoruba movies for my children (aged 7 and 4) and so far, it's been a futile search. Nigerian History in consumable formats for this day and age is scarce. People of my age know very little about our history, talk less of the generations coming behind, many of them born in modern times and cities all over the world. In 2009, History was removed from Nigerian primary and secondary schools' curriculum stating many reasons including the dearth of history teachers. Word has it that it was reintroduced in 2018.

We have an identity challenge that also impacts how we approach the future. We're losing language, norms, and values that should be preserved regardless of the location or flag we may carry. Origin remains origin. Nigeria needs us, and our children, and as such, we should not forget where we came from. If we don't we can retrace our steps, then we can rebuild.

"From generation to generation" offers us a glimpse into what was, what is and what could be as a country. In it, you'll find Nigeria's history (a focus on Yoruba) being told through the eyes of Baba Oladosu Awoyemi, my grand uncle who as an educated young man; had high hopes for Africa working with the government, building a new Nigeria, and now as a octogenarian, is still very hopeful.

In it, you'll find stories that help you and yours understand norms, values, and historical events in Nigeria; which you won't find anywhere else easily. I want my children to read "From Generation to Generation", ask questions about their great grand Uncle, Ile-Ife, Nigeria, and create vivid imaginations of their own place and responsibility to Nigeria and the Yoruba race.

I am also throwing out a challenge here which I hope becomes a trend. Be like Auntie Tobi and Uncle Femi. Pick up your phone, turn on your camera, ask your parents and grandparents questions about history, growing up. Keep it or share it, it's up to you. If you share it, tag it #FromGenerationToGeneration. Either way, I guarantee you would be grateful you captured those valuable moments that might go with them into the beyond.

If you read to this point, you get a bonus poem inspired by JayZ's Forever Young.

On the trips, over dinner, on vacations

The story shall be passed down to generations

With a little ambition, just what Nigeria can become here

And as the father passed the story down to his son's ears

and the son, to the granddaughter and grandson, let's all keep it going.

And our (his)story stays alive and forever green.

- Opeyemi Awoyemi is an entrepreneur and most known for creating Jobberman, Africa's largest job search website. He was born and grew up in Ile-Ife, Nig

CONTENTS

Introduction

We have all heard the saying: "A good man leaves an inheritance for his children's children," but we might not be so familiar with the notion that the legacy a good man leaves behind includes history; history of the family, of course, that goes without saying, but also history of the nation, history of the group of people they belong to, history of our successes and failures, history of where we are from.

Your initial thought might well be that the world is filled with history books, and we have thousands of historians, so why do we need another history lesson? While that is true, most history books aren't written by an old man recounting the tales of his experience to his children and grandchildren. They aren't written in a way that says: "I was there when this happened; this is how I felt and how it affected me as a person, and not just a statistic."

Furthermore, I have noticed a lapse in the understanding of African history in the current generation. Recently, I have found myself in conversations with children who have spent their formative years in Nigeria yet are not educated in the recent history of the nation. My 15-year-old nephew once said to me, "I never knew there was a time when there were good roads in Nigeria". Another recent one was, "Oh! I did not realise there was a telephone service in Nigeria 30 years ago!". 'What! Does this kid live under a rock!' I hear you say.

Just before we pass the buck to generation Z, I must confess my history blind spots as well. I recall reading *Half a Yellow Sun* a few years ago, and all of a sudden, I realised that I knew very little about the Biafra war. Upon realising this, I did a quick poll amongst a few friends, and realised they were in exactly the same boat. So, you see, from generation X right through to the current iGen, we are all guilty of not promoting our African history. Therefore, I hope to use this book to remind us of a historical fact or two about our homeland.

Rather than quote some facts about events of the past, we are going to talk to my dad. Yep! Talk and ask questions. I find it's quicker, simpler and it gets straight to the point, so hopefully it will keep you reading, especially if you find history dry. Just like our last book, *Growing Old Gracefully*, Tobi and I will pick a topic, give our perspective on it, and help drive out a story from our dad, which will hopefully give us an interesting history lesson.

First, let's introduce Dad and get a snippet of what he'll be talking about over the next few chapters:

Hello reader, I am Mr Oladosu Awoyemi (A.K.A) Grandpa, and by the special grace of God, I have lived through eight-and-a-half decades, in which I have been resident in Nigeria, except for a few months spent abroad from time to time. I can therefore claim to be a living witness to events that have taken place for about 75 years, assuming that I would not have been fully aware of events during the first decade, when I was essentially a child. It's my pleasure to pass on what I have witnessed over the years, and I hope you all retell these stories and facts we share here.

Over the next few chapters, as I answer questions from my son and daughter-in-law, I will recall some landmark events which have taken place over the past 75 years. This will cover a wide range of issues, including parenting during my childhood; my experiences through primary, secondary and university education in Nigeria; notable changes in the system over the decades; issues relating to the upbringing of children; social relationships and family matters; and discipline.

I will also shed light on how governance of the nation has evolved from colonial times to Nigerian independence, and the present presidential system, including the evolution of the political system as we know it today. I will give my perspective on the issues of religion, especially the seemingly sharp division between the two major religions, Christianity, and Islam. Has it always been so sharp?

We will be visiting my primary professional constituency, namely Agriculture and Rural Development, and looking at how it has evolved over the decades, examining how the discovery of petroleum has impacted agricultural development in particular, and the economy as a whole.

As far as it is possible, I will make my responses anecdotal to enhance their veracity and relevance to you, the audience. My hope and desire is that you, the reader, get a perspective of what it was like living in an African nation from the colonial era, through the days of prosperity, to the current economic and social turmoil we find ourselves in as a nation. The news and history books will provide a certain perspective but talking to your parents and grandparents will provide the perspective the news will never be able to capture. I should also stress there is something in this book for everybody, from the awkward questions from my grandchildren to the more serious discussion on corruption. This should hopefully shed more light onto your knowledge of Africans, though from a Nigerian perspective.

This book has been written in an interview style to make your reading more enjoyable, and to reflect, as accurately as possible, some of the conversations that led to the topics discussed in the book. Have a good read, and please tell us what you think on the various social media channels.

God Bless,

Oladosu Awoyemi

CHAPTER ONE:

Civic 101: Getting to Know Nigeria

As part of our effort to introduce Nigeria to her own citizens at home and abroad, here are a few facts you should know before delving into the main topics of discussion.

1. The geographical space known as Nigeria was a collection of states which existed as distinct kingdoms, chiefdoms, and diverse ethnic entities. Each was governed by leaders, elected, selected or self-imposed and independent.

2. All entities were amalgamated into one country by the British Government and named Nigeria in the year 1914. Racially, the vast majority are negroes, but descendants of Arabs also form a significant portion of the indigenes.

3. Over two-hundred languages are spoken, not to mention dialects. Among the tribal groups are Yoruba, Hausa, Fulani, Igbo, Kanuri, Efik, Ibibio, Tiv, Jukun, Edo, etc.

4. The population is estimated to be around 200 million, and is growing at about 2% per annum, making Nigeria the most populous African nation and the seventh most populous in the world.

5. Nigeria is basically an agrarian country, with about 65% of the population engaging in farming, fishing, animal husbandry and related activities. The major food crops are maize, guinea corn, millet, yam cassava, beans etc. Nigeria has the capacity to produce all her food requirements. The export crops are cocoa, palm oil and kernels, rubber, groundnut, cotton, and other minor crops, such as benniseed, soya beans, etc. In the past, animal hides and skins were also exported.

6. The Nigerian extensive coastal waters and lagoons were once very rich in fishery resources and crustaceans, especially shrimp.

7. Nigeria is the eight largest exporter of petroleum in the world, and about 80% of the foreign exchange earnings come from petroleum, including gas.

8. Nigeria has substantial deposits of coal, columbite, bitumen, tin, iron ore and even gold spread all over the geographical zones.

9. Nigeria is located mainly in the tropics and has two main seasons: the rainy season and the dry season. The two seasons vary in quantity and spread from the coastal region to the semi desert in the north. The quantity of rain varies from 50cm in the arid north to as much as 200cm per annum in the coastal region.

10. After amalgamation into a single country in 1914, Nigeria was divided administratively into three regions:

the Eastern, Western and Northern Regions. Each region was divided into provinces for administrative purposes.

11. The British introduced the parliamentary form of government with a bi-cameral assembly, the House of Representatives, and the House of Chiefs in the regions. There was also a federal legislature, but political power and autonomy resided with the regional governments.

12. On October 1st, 1960, Nigeria became an independent nation but maintained the British parliamentary system.

13. In 1966, the military staged a coup d'etat and drastically changed the form of government to a unitary system, with ultimate power residing with the head of the Federal Military Government.

14. Then, over a period of about 20 years, the three political regions were subdivided by military fiat into what is now 36 states, with a Federal Capital Territory, each with its own House of Assembly, but the House of Chiefs was abolished.

15. Subsequently, the American presidential system was adopted, with three arms of the government: the National Assembly, called the Legislature (this comprises of the House of Representatives and Senate); the President and his Ministers, called the Executive; and then the Judiciary.

16. The final step in the political evolution of Nigeria was the establishment of Local Government Councils, which evolved from the old Native Authorities that existed during the colonial era. There are 774 Local Government Council areas in the country.

17. Nigeria is governed under a constitution that defines the responsibilities and power of the federal, state, and local governments. The constitution is currently going through a third revision due to perceived imperfections in its current form.

18. The British judicial system was adopted, and state and federal high courts were established. The federal court also has a court of appeal, to which cases could be referred. Initially, cases decided at the appeal court could be appealed to the Privy Council, the highest in the United Kingdom, but then Nigeria became a republic in 1963. The Nigeria Supreme Court was established and became the apex court, thus severing connection with the Privy Council.

19. Another interesting fact about Nigeria is that Nigerians are among the most dispersed people in the world, with over 15 million of them living in virtually all countries, especially in Europe and North America.

20. Nigerians are among the most educated Africans. For instance, the number of Nigerian medical doctors operating in other countries is greater than those

remaining at home, with high concentrations in South Africa, USA, Arab countries, and the United Kingdom. Generally, Nigerians are hilarious people, very vibrant and highly adaptable, and are even able to maintain an optimistic outlook in dire circumstances.

21. Nigerians, and notably the women folk, are among the most enterprising people on Earth, hence you will find Nigerian traders and artisans all over West Africa and indeed all over the world.

22. 'Nollywood', the colloquial term for the Nigerian movie industry, employs over a million people, making it one of the largest film industries in the world.

23. Nigeria is a foremost sporting nation, particularly in soccer (football) and athletics. There are Nigerians playing football in every major soccer league in the world.

24. Nigeria has a great future ahead. As peace returns, Nigeria will pick up momentum and will rank among the greatest economies in the world.

Hopefully, the above facts have whetted your appetite and you are ready for the main course of the book!

CHAPTER TWO:

The One Eyed Cane Master

Tobi: Whenever Femi and I reminisce about our childhood memories and how things are so different for our children, it feels like we were children growing up a century ago. Growing up in the broadband, super-fast information age, our children's lives are the complete opposites of Femi's and mine. For instance, I remember having a pen pal as a young girl. I would write to my pal in another school. Even though we were just several hours' drive away, it still took a week for my letters to arrive. Then, I'd have to wait another week-plus before a reply arrived in the mail. When I compare myself to my daughter, it makes me think I am much more patient than she is. After all, she only has to send an email to her email pal, and a response would be there in minutes.

When I think of you growing up in rural Nigeria in the 1940s and 50s, it makes me wonder how easy I must have had it as a child growing up in the 1980s. In your case, you would have learned to be a lot more patient, no doubt. If my letters took over a week to be delivered, how long did yours take? Did you have running water in the house? One of my biggest frustrations growing up in Nigeria, and arguably this is the same for most Africans, was (you guessed it!) NEPA (National Electric Power Authority, for my non-Nigerian readers). This means power cuts, which were all too frequent. I am wondering, did you have electricity in the first place? So, Dad, what was life like growing up in your time?

Dad: I grew up in Ilé-Ifẹ̀. As you know, Ifẹ̀ is a Yoruba settlement that dates back several centuries. We can talk about the history of Yoruba's in our next book. Our lives in Ifẹ̀ was simple, and I got to live through a lot of changes as a child. Our lives were governed by simple, traditional practices regarding family, land ownership and transfer, marriage and funeral rites, arrival of new babies and their naming and identification within families and clans, divorce and remarriage, widowhood, and treatment of widows, etc. And this was a similar case for a lot of the African cultures and different clans.

Let's talk marriage as our first example of how things have changed, up to 70 years ago, marriage was a serious family affair. Parents were involved in the selection of a wife or husband. Sometimes, parents, through strong interfamily ties, selected a husband for their daughter on the basis of long years of cordial relationship. The children were simply called and introduced to each other, and subsequently, payment of a dowry and other traditional rites were performed, mostly at the expense of the grooms' parents, and very little money was involved. Materials such as kola nuts, honey, yam, and cloth were bought for the bride at a simple ceremony.

Tobi: That's interesting, the men had to foot the bill for the wedding, wow! I am sure many ladies out there would love to revert to that tradition!

Dad: In some cases, the man may have been studying or working abroad, and the wife was sent to join him. The man would take a photograph of the lady, which had been sent previously, to identify her at the port of disembarkation. On identifying her with the picture, she would follow him to his residence, and both would start living together as husband and wife thereafter.

Tobi: Even though I have heard of this tradition many times before, Dad, it sounds like a movie as you say it. How can you see someone from a picture and that's it!!! You fall in love! What if they didn't look like they did in the photograph with all the makeup and pristine hair, etc? What if the man said no, would she have had to return on the next flight home?

Dad: Somehow, the arrangement worked to the satisfaction of both parties most of the time. There would have been a lot of preparation and courting by both families, such that the arrangement went without a hitch most of the time. This is probably because the main concern in those days was character rather than physical beauty.

With the advance of Western education, the responsibility for finding or selecting marriage partners shifted to the boys and girls, but this was still subject to approval from parents.

In my case, two scenarios played out. Firstly, when I was in my final year at the university, I met a girl who was a school mate and friend of my younger sister, and we agreed to become friends. As the relationship progressed, I started to visit her at her home. The mother, who probably knew my family, readily welcomed me, but the father, who did not approve of the relationship, took a very unusual step. Instead of telling his daughter to terminate the relationship, he came to my own father to tell me to keep away from his daughter, as he would not betroth her to my family. Needless to say, that friendship had to end and I later learned that her father planned to give her to the son of his friend and boss.

Tobi: That's an amazing story, Daddy! You'll excuse my hysteria. That sounds so cliché: Girl's dad tells the boyfriend's father, "Tell your son to stay away from my daughter". Did your father scold you?

Dad: Not at all, my father had a way with ladies, but, at the same time, he was also quite traditional and strict, so there was no going against him on this one, or most things for that matter.

In the second scenario, I met another pretty lady, and after a short period of courtship, we brought her mother into the picture. In accordance with the practice in Yoruba land in those days, the lady's mother carried out some investigations about my family. She even sent someone to Ifẹ to check on my background. Apparently, she must have been very pleased with her findings because she became very welcoming and encouraged her daughter to accept me fully. This is how we became married for 40 years with five children to show for it.

These two stories illustrate the crucial role of parents in marriage in the past. The situation now is that most children hardly involve their parents in their choice of marriage partners and whatever follows subsequently. I think the role of families cannot be overestimated in preparing for marriage.

Tobi: Sticking with the topic of how families operated back in the day, what role did families play in raising children? We often say it takes a village to raise a child. Did you live that proverb?

Dad: The role of families, especially mothers, did not end with the marriage of their daughter. They continued to play the role of counsellor and midwife. They stayed with their daughter for about six to eight weeks after the birth of her first child, to train and help her in raising the new baby. That has not changed much today, and it is a great tradition I would encourage.

Another old family tradition, which is no longer done, was for a young mother to send her child of about two years old over to live with her parents, to free her to pursue some economic activities, or to have another baby, or further her education. The child would live with the grandparents until it was time to go to primary school. There were no crèches or nursery schools in those days, so the child was nursed by grandparents, aunties, and other family members, who often resided close to each other. Nowadays, even grandparents are too busy pursuing their own life goals, and modern parents also don't believe that their own parents can bring their child up to modern standards.

Tobi: You make it sound like family was all perfect in your time. Did the relationships always work out?

Dad: Relationship challenges are as old as when man and woman were first created. We also had our unique challenges at the time. Take divorce and remarriage, for example. Though not very common, the traditions still made room for that. Because marriage involved the union of families of couples, divorce was not easy in the past, as the families went to great lengths to dissuade the couple from coming apart. If one of them, despite all efforts, decided to opt out of the relationship, there were native courts where a spouse could go and make a complaint. On hearing their cases, if the wife was the guilty party, she was made to refund the dowry paid on her to her husband. If she had children for the man, the refund of the dowry was waived, but the man usually got custody of the children, unless the child was too young to be separated from the mother. The issues of maintenance costs or alimony usually did not apply in those days. Under native law and custom, the father was the owner of the child and could take the child away from the mother, after the period of childhood or at about five years of age.

Tobi: Wow, it is interesting to know that, at some point, the dads had automatic custody of the children, and I find

13

it really hilarious that the lady had to return the dowry, considering some of the items were perishables.

Dad: Where separation was due to the early death of a spouse, the traditions have also changed significantly, when compared to today's African society. When an old man died, his wives, who were most likely to be old, also remained widows for the rest of their lives. The younger wives, if they were still of childbearing age, were inherited by the oldest son.

Tobi: What! What kind of tradition is that Dad? I can understand handing over a wife to a son as a mother to look after him, but how can she be handed over as a wife? I feel for such women, oh my gosh!

Dad: Hold on my dear daughter, let me give you another interesting shocker, and you need to sit down for this one.

Tobi: Ok, Dad, shall I close my ears for this one?

Dad: Sometimes, an old man, while still alive, would hand over his young wife to his oldest son to take over the role of a husband, so that the young woman could receive proper care, but he would also take over the raising of the woman's children.

I see you are speechless, so let me explain the rationale for this. It's quite simple really. Most of our mothers were quite dependent on our fathers at this time; therefore, an old man getting too ill to sustain and maintain his family would have meant the family suffered. So, therefore, tradition provided this means to take care of the woman, who was now a part of the man's family.

For the younger men, the rules were even more complex. You would say shocking by today's standards. When a man died young or in mid-life, usually his wife was transferred to his younger brother. She, however, could choose to go and marry another man or remain in the family to raise her children.

Tobi: Daddy, I am so so glad you just said she could choose, and I hope most of the women in this situation chose to leave and remarry.

Dad: I wish I could give you the answer to ease the expression on your face, but you must remember, our mothers were born into this tradition. It was all they knew, so for a lot of them, it only seemed normal, plus it guaranteed their safety and security.

Gradually, these traditions changed, of course, and they also had their complexities. In the above example, the young man could choose not to accept to take over his brother's wife, because he could not cope with additional responsibilities. And there were other complexities, such as which position the woman would hold. For example, would she now be the first wife, as she might be older? What happened to the man's estate was also another area of difficulty. All these made it quite challenging to administer some of these traditions, and they faded away as more and more of us became educated in Western cultures and traditions.

The important thing to understand is that traditions evolve. Most are man-made, so are subject to change over time. Some of the more interesting changes I have seen in my lifetime include those to inheritance of land. At present, people own land and pass it on to their children, but it wasn't always so. The practice in the olden days was that land returned to the pool of the clan when the cultivator died, but his children would continue to enjoy the right of use. If the children, as in recent times, chose not to farm the land and it returned to fallow, then the leadership of the clan could allocate it to another member of the clan. In case of urban land, ownership was primarily established by the family member who had legitimately put some permanent structures on the land. Surveys and formal conveyance by the State Government conferred permanent ownership to the individual. With regard to other assets, such as houses, business enterprises and cash inheritance, this was from the father to all children. It was shared along mother lines called *'idi-igi'*. Both sons and daughters had equal rights to their father's properties, though this practice differed among other tribes. Usually, elders in the clan would preside over the sharing of assets if invited to do so.

Tobi: Let's talk about other areas of life back in the day.

Dad: Communication is another area where we have seen big changes. When I was growing up, there were very few telephones in the whole of Ilé-Ifẹ̀. Up to the early 1950s, telephone services were very rudimentary. Only the elites of that time, such as a traditional ruler, senior chiefs, wealthy produce merchants and the handful of doctors and lawyers, which in Ifẹ̀ could not have been more than 50, had access to telephone services. We had to go through the nearest telephone exchange 50km away, at Oshogbo, to get to any part of Nigeria. Telephone service to overseas countries was virtually non-existent. Even as late as the 1970s, one had to go to the Nigerian Telecommunications (NITEL) service station to call an overseas subscriber, with the assistance of an operator.

We did a lot of walking in those days, as there were no means of transport, such as taxis or motorcycles as we have today. So, in my case, I walked 3km to and from my primary school every day, come rain or sun. If you needed to send information to a friend or family member miles away, you simply walked. Up till the late 1940s, information to the public was disseminated from the paramount ruler of a town through town criers. They went through the town, stopping at intervals to sound a gong. On hearing the gong, people came to hear whatever message the authorities wanted to pass to the populace, and then those who heard the information first-hand helped spread it to others, and it was quite effective.

Tobi: How effective could that have been, Dad? Didn't the information end up being Chinese whispers? Wasn't it diluted by the time it was passed on as second or third-hand information?

Dad: I really cannot figure out why it worked so well, but it was certainly an effective mode of communication. In any case, most of the messages were simple instructions to the populace.

This started to change in the early 1950s. The Western Nigeria Government had a radio service for which reception boxes were purchased and installed in homes. Government passed information to people through these boxes. It was called Government Rediffusion Service.

Tobi: That sounds really interesting, almost like what you would hear of in an old communist state. How did you know when to switch on the service and when the Government had some details to pass on?

Dad: The service was left on permanently. The broadcasting station opened at 6am and closed at 8pm. Later on, possibly in the late 1950s, short-wave radio came into service, making it possible to own radio receiving sets and tune in to radio broadcasting stations outside of Nigeria.

Tobi: Let's talk about an area that's close to my heart, Dad.

Dad: Let me guess! Education? I wondered when you were going to ask about that, being the teacher of the family. So, let me tell you about my school days. I liked going to school. It was a privilege. I enjoyed learning, even to this day, and I am very grateful for the education I received from the old Western Region in the 1940s and 50s. Our teachers were well-trained products of teacher training colleges, highly committed and highly regarded, and they were permitted to maintain a high standard of discipline.

Tobi: Permitted to maintain discipline? I think I know what that means.

Dad: Yes, as you can imagine, the teachers in those days used the cane generously on recalcitrant pupils, so much so that we feared them more than our parents.

I recall with some trepidation having a teacher who was blind in one eye. When caning pupils, he used to say, "*Oju Aanu tifo tika loku*," which means, "The eye of mercy is gone and the one remaining is the eye of wickedness".

Tobi: What! That sounds so terrible, Dad.

Femi: Dad, I know I shouldn't be laughing, but I am literally rolling on the floor with laughter here. A one-eyed teacher with no eye for mercy! How did he see you? Couldn't you just stay on the side of his blind spot.

Dad: He was quite fearsome, so no one dared mess with him. Frankly, it made us all sit up. Discipline and hard work were the order of the day during my time. We had weekly tests in arithmetic, and the number of canes you received was according to your score. Eight over ten received only one stroke of the cane, while two over ten received six lashes.

Femi: I am in hysterics again here, Dad! I can't help but imagine there would have been some boys who got the cane daily. It would have been like a routine.

Tobi: Can I just add, as an educator, I don't believe in corporal punishment.

Dad: This treatment made us work harder in the study of arithmetic, to reduce the chance of being flogged with the cane, and this certainly played a part in helping me score a high credit in the subject in the then West African School Certificate Examination in later years. That's not to say I condone such methods of teaching; that was just how it was for us at that time.

Another good teaching practice I recall was how our teachers in standard six selected the brighter pupils and gave us extra coaching to enhance our performance in gaining entrance to the better secondary schools in those days. These included Government College Ibadan, Kings College Lagos, etc. This enabled St Stephen School Modakeke to send many pupils to these schools for several years, until some policy changes in the education sector ended selection of some schools for the special high-standard schools. Teachers provided a coaching service free of charge for the joy of setting their pupils up for a better future. I certainly benefitted from this service. I gained entry to Government College Ibadan. At that time, teachers at GCI were mainly British citizens, and the school was like a typical British boarding school. The teachers were all university graduates, highly disciplined and well-motivated.

Tobi: That sounds like it was the golden age of education in Nigeria; it almost sounds idyllic.

Dad: It was certainly a privilege to be educated under that system. Some of the disciplines I imbibed then, like reading a book a week, mental arithmetic, etc, still help me in my day-to-day life at 86 years old. That said, I wouldn't say that was the golden age of education. For me, the golden age was when education became free in the old Western Region. I am sure you will agree with me that all children should be given basic education for free. It is the number-one determinant of life chances for that child and their family.

One of the little things I remember from my primary school days was that ball point pens, popularly called biros, were not yet in use, so you had to dip the nib of your pen into an ink well. School desks had holes, into which the ink well was placed, so each pupil could reach it. You would buy readymade ink in small bottles with the trademark Quink, or buy blue or black ink powder and mix with water. It got quite messy at times, and careless pupils would often soil their exercise books and clothes. 1 doubt if children these days have seen an inkwell, except in movies.

Tobi: I'd always assumed school was free all along, so it seems it was paid for at a point. Surely, that would have been a deterrent to many families at that time.

Dad: Oh yes, we did have to pay for school, though my secondary school fees was only £35 per annum at the time. That's equivalent to £1,200 in today's money. That was still out of reach for many. It was value for money though. For that price, we were supplied books and stationery, school uniform for classes, and sanitation work clothes, which was called fatigue dress in those days, and even an outfit for Sunday church.

Tobi: Oh wow! Dad, that sounds like an upmarket school to me, all for £1,200. What a bargain!

Dad: The value was really in the education that we received. All school activities were compulsory, even going to church on Sunday for Christians, and to the mosque on Friday for Muslims. We had to take good care of schoolbooks, because they were collected at the end of the year for use by the next class. Any infraction of school rules was severely punished. The rampant indiscipline of the present day, including cultism, use of hard drugs and other deviant behaviours, were non-existent. Ordinary cheating in school-term examination could earn a student outright expulsion. We lived highly regimented lives, with time allotted for classroom attendance, dining, studies, sports, sanitation, and hobbies. No wonder the school produced ready materials for the universities. Invariably, most of them later turned out to be leaders in many areas of life, including top civil servants, judicial officers, professors in various disciplines, etc. These outcomes confirm the doctrine that foundation is very critical in every area of human endeavour.

Needless to say, my admission to the university was a matter of course, and I was privileged to attend the most prestigious university in Africa at the time, University College Ibadan (a College of University of London), which was the one and only university in Nigeria in 1957, when l entered university. We faced very stiff competition to gain admission, as the total student population was about 2,500. The female population was less than 10%; this is in sharp contrast to the present, where the female population in some universities in Eastern Nigeria is over 60%.

Femi: My turn to ask a question, please. It seems to me the women in the university at that time would have been in extremely high demand!! For every 10 guys there was one woman!

Dad: Can we have a more serious question from Tobi, please.

Tobi: Yes please, let's discuss social life. What was it like on a typical Friday evening, or weekend evening, while children were not at school? What did they do at home with parents?

Dad: After the day's economic activities, people of the 1940s had various ways of recreation. Parents interacted with children by sitting outside the home to tell folk tales, which was passed from generation to generation. They told riddles and jokes. There was a lot of time to spend together in the early evenings. The elderly men, who were mostly farmers and hunters, sang dirges and recited poems in praise of ancient heroes. We also played local games, such as Ayo, draft, card games and, later on, Ludo. Those evenings also afforded parents the opportunity to teach their grown-up children the use of herbs and other plant parts to treat diseases.

Tobi: Do you remember any such poems, riddles or tales?

Dad: One of the popular folk tales was about the race between the hare and the tortoise. The hare, being the faster animal, was comfortably ahead of the tortoise, so he decided to take a short rest, thinking he had the race in the bag and didn't have to break a sweat. Unfortunately, he dozed off, and the tortoise caught up with him and won the race. Hence the common saying: 'Slow and steady wins the race.'

Let me tell you another for good measure. You must have heard of the story of two twin brothers. They went to the oracle to know what the future had in store. Mr Oracle told Taiye (common Yoruba name for the twin that was born first), "You are going to be king of your clan when you grow up". Mr Oracle told Kehinde (common Yoruba name for the twin born second), "You will be an ordinary man in your village". So, Taiye started to live the life of a king, like the proverbial prodigal son, while Kehinde went to a distant land to set up a farm and became prosperous. When the Oba (king) of the village joined his ancestors, it coincided with the period of famine, so the villagers needed a new *Oba* who could support them, and Taiye didn't fit the bill, only in name. Soon, news reached the villagers that their other prince, Kehinde, had become a prosperous farmer, so they sent for him to come with all his wealth and rule over them. The lesson here is that the wise, in most cases, will become rich and rule over the foolish.

Tobi: Thanks for those, Dad. I'll add them to my repertoire of folk tales I can also pass on to the children.

Tell us more about social life back in the day. I am guessing there were no night clubs or restaurants or bars at that time, so how did the teens and young adults hang out?

Dad: I fondly remember, in those days, the food markets in urban centres operated daily, mainly in the evenings, from about 5pm to 8pm. These evening markets were a social rendezvous for the young folk and for choosing future partners. The parents knew the score, as they had done the same in their own time, so it wasn't discouraged. Those evening markets have mostly disappeared, probably for security reasons. It was fascinating to see hundreds of small lamps fueled by palm oil, or kerosene lamps, lighting the wares displayed by women, as there was no electricity in Ifè at this time.

Entertainment gradually developed in Nigeria, just like the other industries we see now, starting from the mid-1940s. When I was a lad, the Ogunde Theatre party had been formed. They staged plays designed to teach life lessons, while also entertaining, so they moved from town to town, using town halls or secondary school assembly halls where available. The gate fees were affordable to encourage many families to attend. Other theatre parties, such as Duro Ladipo and Moses Olaiya A.K.A Baba Sala, followed later, thus laying the foundation for the present-day Nigerian theatre.

I fondly recall the early cinema. The shows were staged in open fields by commercial firms to advertise their products, using projectors. I recall that the film producing company was Pearl and Dean Ltd, while Lever Brothers and other British traders supplied advertisements. The main purpose of those films was to advertise their products, but they usually accompanied this with some theatrical plays and dancing.

Tobi: That's quite interesting. The cinemas of today still follows the same principle; the first 20 minutes of any movie are commercials and a Pearl and Dean intro.

Dad: By the late 1940s/early 50s, formal cinema houses were built in Ibadan by Arab and Lebanese companies, which hired films to entertain people on a daily basis. Initially, they were European films, including great films such as *Julius Caesar, Romeo and Juliet*, etc, but these were displaced by Indian films, which were very popular among largely illiterate people, who could not understand films with complex plots and themes.

Tobi: I remember watching Indian films as a child on VHS tapes. Somehow, I can't imagine those films could have been around long before I was born. So, were these in English? Did most of the populace speak a form of pidgin English at the time, or did they just relay the movies in Punjab, and the audiences picked up the plot along the way?

Dad: The Indian movies of the time were filled with music and theatrical dancing, so this was the main source of entertainment and fun for the audiences. Though the movies were translated into English, you could follow the plot without the translation. They were great fun for us and a good introduction to cinema.

 Before we close this chapter, I thought I should

mention a note to our younger readers about twins in Nigeria, based on the folk tale I mentioned. Most twins in Yoruba land were called Taiye and Kehinde, and did you know that Nigeria and the Yoruba tribe have one of the highest rates of twins per thousand families in the world? The name Taiye literally means 'the one who tasted of the world first', hence the name is given to the first twin to come out of the mother's womb. Legend says that Taiye usually comes to check out the world, then sends a message to his or her twin, Kehinde, to come along if he/she finds the world to be a nice place. Kehinde means 'the one who came out second', and this is the name usually given to the twin who comes out second from the womb.

An interesting practice amongst parents of twins in those days was to consult the oracle concerning the future of the twins. Sometimes, the oracle would declare that the mother of the twins should go around the town dancing to entertain people, so she would hire a drummer, and she would sing and dance. In return, people would offer the twins gifts of food, clothing and cash. This practice helped the parents of twins to raise the children for up to two or three years without financial pressure.

Femi: What if the mother was a bad dancer, would anyone still give her gifts? And why didn't the dad also dance? Seems a bit unfair! What if the mother refused the oracle's instructions?

Dad: Not everyone followed the instructions of the oracle, especially those who were from wealthier families who didn't require the financial and social support, and so, gradually, over the years, the tradition faded away.

CHAPTER THREE:

Independence to Dependence

Femi: Picture this, Dad: you walk into a Nigerian bar or restaurant and overhear the conversation of a group of men, let's say their average age is over 40 years. They are all shouting and expressing their expert views with such conviction, you wonder why that situation still exists if they are such passionate folks. Most of us would have seen or experienced this scenario. This group of men are talking about the economy; corruption; how bad things have become; how the Nigerian currency, the naira, has fallen from an almost equal parring to 600 naira to a pound. They talk about what to do about the situation and how they would make a difference if they were in power. A few hours later, after a few bowls of pepper soup and Guinness, the pitch of the conversation pipes down as they digress to more sociable topics, like sports, only to resume the same discussion with equal vigor the next time they meet.

Whenever I am in those circles, I often get lost in thought; thoughts of the time before the men started having those sorts of conversations about the economy. I would have been about seven, maybe eight years old. I used to go down the street to buy Bigdeep. You probably do not remember this, Dad. Bigdeep was a vanilla ice cream covered in chocolate, held together by a wooden stem running through the middle. We call this a Magnum in this generation. The cost for Bigdeep must have been 50 or 60 kobo at the time. Mum would treat me to this a few times a week, but I suspect you were never aware of how much of that stuff I ate, otherwise I would have been banned!

I reminisce with fondness about this novel time in my life. I remember Bigdeep got more expensive though; from 50 or 60 kobo, I recall prices went up to 1 naira and beyond. When I think back to this period, I realise a couple of things happened. Firstly, Mum didn't allow me to buy my favourite ice cream as often as I had become accustomed to. From a few times a week, this turned to once a week or once in a while. Secondly, on the rare occasions I was allowed to buy Bigdeep, I was met with even more disappointment. The Mama (that's what I called the old lady who sold the ice cream from a freezer outside her home) would smile at my little face and give me the disappointing news, "Bigdeep is out of stock". "Why?" I would retort. "Why!" My eight-year-old mind never really understood her response though: "Austerity," or in her language *"ko si oja,"* which translated as "The market/the business is slow".

30 years on, I realise what must have happened to my beloved Bigdeep. UAC (the major ice-cream manufacturer at the time) couldn't source the raw materials for the ice cream. They either didn't have the foreign currency to source the ingredients and/or they didn't have the parts for the machinery needed for ice cream, and so they probably discontinued it and other products which weren't essential commodities. Furthermore, with prices tripling from the initial stable costs, they would have lost most of their repeat customers, like myself, whose frugal mums took ice cream off the food menu after a while. I would argue ice cream is an essential commodity for a seven-year-old, but let's focus on the topic at hand.

The Bigdeep episode is one of my experiences of an economic downturn, hyperinflation, currency devaluation, or whatever technical economic jargon we want to dress this with. For many, it would have been so much worse. Indeed, some might read this and think, 'For crying out loud! Get over the Bigdeep dude! People starved through this time. 'Needless to say, that's one of the things that stuck with me as a child.

I am pretty certain that my ice-cream story can be told many times over in most African countries. Independence is achieved, the economy starts to grow, and then the growth is stunted by economic policies that more or less reinstate dependence on the former colonial masters. And that's not changed much, even today.

So, Dad, let's talk about you and how this affected you, and others like yourself, a professional at the height of your career during this period, having enjoyed the trappings of foreign education. At some point, the currency you spent daily ranked at par with the major Western currencies. You probably had thousands in your bank account at any given time. Things must have been very good for society in general. But I am guessing one Friday you had thousands in your account, only to realise that it was only worth a few hundred as you awoke on the Monday morning. How did you survive that?

Dad: That's a good question, Femi. First, let me make it clear that the devaluation of the currency didn't just happen over a weekend. It was gradual, so people adjusted over a period of time. That said, it was still a challenge for people like me, and it was a disaster for those who were already on the fringe, those with lower incomes. That era you just described spelt economic ruin for many families and businesses. Indeed, that era continues today. Inflation in Nigeria is still at an all-time high. Our currency has never really recovered, and unemployment has never been higher. The only difference with this generation is that we experienced the economic downturn first-hand, while most of our children of today have never experienced an economic boom. They have only ever known a weak economy.

To maintain a consistent starting point in the consideration of the major issues in the Nigerian social and economic life, let us go back in time, as we have done with other topics, and consider the place of money in Nigeria from about 70 years ago, and how it has fared over time. In 1973, Nigeria transited from the old West African currency, which was in use in former territories under British colonial rule in West Africa, namely Nigeria, Ghana (formally Gold Coast), Sierra-Leone and Gambia, and adopted the naira as its own national currency.

Femi: Is it not ironic that we are now talking about a single currency in West Africa?

Dad: At the beginning, one pound sterling was equivalent to two naira, due to a very strong economy based on the export of cocoa, palm kernel, rubber, cotton, groundnut, chili pepper, benniseed, etc. By the time the decline of export crops set in, the export of petroleum had begun. This kept the currency very strong until the mid-1980s. At the time of my retirement in 1987, my gratuity for 32 years' service was only N36,000.00. A brand-new Mercedes Benz 200 was selling for about N12,000.

The International Monetary Fund (IMF), the World Bank and others in their group started to raise alarm that the Nigerian currency was overvalued. Then, they started to pressurise Nigeria and other countries in similar situations to adopt the Structural Adjustment Programme (SAP), and they began to make it a condition for obtaining loans and credit from these world bodies. When Nigeria succumbed to their pressure, a steady decline in the exchange rate of the naira began, and it has gotten now to an incredible rate of about N600 plus to the pound sterling. New cars, which used to cost N10,000 to purchase, now cost millions of naira.

Over the course of the last 70 years, our attitude as a people towards the acquisition of money has changed. 70 years ago, very few Nigerians could be regarded as rich men that had cash and assets in excess of a million naira. The source of wealth for such men was well known. They were merchants, industrialists, and owners of publishing houses. They were highly regarded as honourable men. Names such as Alhaji

Dantata, Chief T. A. Odutola, Chief Odumagwu Ojukwu and Chief Okotieboh readily come to mind.

In the early 1960s, another set of millionaires began to emerge. They belonged to the political class, and they got their money through government contracts, from main-line ministries, government parastatals and military contracts. These rent seekers got rich with minimum sweat, and so the real moral value began to fall rapidly. They went on spending sprees, buying cars, landed properties, going on holidays abroad, and they instigated the massive importation of consumer goods from abroad. This scale of spending further aggravated the rate of decline of the naira. Ostentatious living became the order of the day.

Fast forward to the late 1980s/90s, when young men, wanting to be like their older brothers, joined the reckless search for wealth by engaging in criminal activities, including dealing in drugs, and duping foreigners through spurious business transactions, known locally as 419, and later on, Yahoo Yahoo, primarily through the internet. Nigeria's image abroad became seriously damaged, to the extent that holders of Nigerian passports were often embarrassed abroad.

Femi: Just a moment, Dad. That's a very interesting perspective I haven't heard before. The new millionaires would have made importation and the use of foreign goods the object of desire for everyone, so the more everyone wanted clothes and goods, combined with the declining exports, our currency just went into free fall.

Dad: That's correct. It's a basic economic principle. If you only consume imported goods and you don't export, you'll become broke. There are other factors, such as a surge in population, and the fact that our local companies couldn't meet the domestic demand, coupled with a slowdown in manufacturing. All these factors brewed the perfect storm for economic crisis in the 1980s.

We are all aware and suffer the consequences of this daily. The state of public infrastructure and social services, like education and health, remains seriously underdeveloped, and the irony is it's irrespective of social class; this still affects everyone.

Another consequence of the severe devaluation of the naira is that the remuneration of public servants has not been adjusted adequately to compensate them for the real value of their services. Thus, the civil servant and indeed the average citizen is poorer today than he was five decades ago.

In an effort to stem this ugly trend, the Nigerian Government established various strategies to help fight fraud and promote the ability for Nigerians to conduct legitimate business. One of the recent ones is the Economic and Financial Crimes Commission EFCC. The commission has succeeded to some extent in checking financial crimes, but we still have a long way to go to bring sanity to the system. The most disturbing aspect is the involvement of highly placed public servants in misappropriating public funds on a large scale, and the failure of the judicial system to stem the tide by recovering the loot and jailing the culprits. Some cases have been going on for a decade.

The youth of this nation have an up-hill task to reverse the decadence, but they are beginning to wake up now. I am seeing more and more youth pledging allegiance and boasting about being Nigerian, especially the ones in the arts, entertainment and in the technology sectors. I believe that will spread to other sectors of society as well.

As pride in our nation starts to resurge, so the trend for preference for foreign goods will decline. As exports increase again, so will the value of the currency. The more valuable the currency is, the more clout we have in organisations such as the World Bank, UN and the EU. It is very much like any other aspect of society; what you bring to the table in terms of financial support, logistics and technology determines what doors open and who listens to you. I have first-hand experience, having worked with some of the above organisations for many years. Very few African countries contributed much, with the exception of South Africa, therefore the African nations were usually dictated to, and considering the heads of most of these organisations are from the developed world, it can almost seem like we have gone from independence back to dependence.

I wouldn't do this topic any justice if I did not talk about solutions in this chapter. While there are many solutions, some complex, some simple, to this issue of our currency, I will only address the one about which I know a thing or two.

I am a firm believer that a nation that can feed itself can defend itself from outside interference and manipulation. You can apply that to other areas of the economy as well, but let's focus on farming. History of warfare tells us that economic blockage is one of the most effective and brutal strategies for winning a war. We saw this used in our civil war. A family, an army, a nation that's starved cannot fight a war. The reverse of that is a nation that's well fed can compete internationally. If Maslow's number-one law is satisfied, the remainder can then follow.

With such a huge population in Nigeria, and Africa

as a whole, agriculture should be one of our weapons of economic independence. And there are simple steps to take towards this. These include making agricultural land readily available. This is the Government incentivising commercial farmers with long land leases free of charge or at a nominal fee, then gradually reducing the importation of certain food items. We have seen that with rice recently. That is a step in the right direction. The farmers will be encouraged to grow these domestically, and, you know what, there is nothing more encouraging to a farmer than when he knows his crops will be consumed by his people. Within 10 to 15 years, or five life cycles of certain crops, the farmers would have become a lot more proficient, not just in growing the crops, but other sectors of farming would have developed alongside, such as processing, packaging, storage, transportation, preservation, logistics, etc. It's a vast value chain that creates sustainable jobs for generations. As we say in Nigeria, "Man must wak," meaning 'We all have to eat'.

Let me illustrate this with some figures. As a young agriculturalist in the 1960s, I was heavily influenced by our export capability as a country, and the impact on jobs and livelihoods. I was also very saddened as this started to shrink over the decades. The below figures drive home this point:

The Peak Years of Nigerian Export Crops

Crops	Year	Tonnage
Cocoa	1970/71	302,400
Palm kernels	1964/65	457,400
Groundnut	1966/67	1,042,800
Seed cotton	1969/70	274,800

And then, compare this to 10 years later. Have a look at groundnut as an example. That is a drop of 100% in export capacity.

Lowest Year of Nigerian Export Crops

Crop	Year	Tonnage
Cocoa	1976/77	120,900
Palm kernels	1977/78	116,500
Groundnut	1973/74	44,000
Seed cotton	1975/76	70,100

Here's my point. If we do not focus on agricultural exports, and only focus on imports, the results will be inevitable. For each ton you export, there are tens of thousands of jobs and mouths being fed. The produce value chain has not changed much in 70years, and it goes somewhat like this; the retail merchants who are often women, go from village to village to buy produce from farmers using standardised measuring baskets, then they bulk the produce and transport it to bigger villages and towns to sell to middlemen who pay by weight. Most middlemen have small

'Avery' scales to weigh the produce and they in turn, would sell to produce merchants, who would sell in tons to exporters after grading. This is a three to four-tier marketing chain. All this helped create a vast economic value chain that sustains thousands of towns and villages, and it can get even bigger with the right focus.

Mind you, there is no such thing as a fully independent nation, just as there is no such thing as a fully independent person. An adult will still have some dependence on his aged parents, their wisdom, direction, etc, and the parents will have some dependence on the grown child, such as company, medical support, etc. As a nation, and talking about Africans now, we must continue to strive to eat what we grow, and grow what we eat, and then import the delicacies and the items we are unable to grow. That's the only path to semi-independence or independence that allows us to take control of our destiny.

Femi: In other words, Dad, I need to tell your grandchildren to stop eating Kellogg's cornflakes and swap them for Ogi and akara; stop eating red apples and swap them for paw paw; stop eating Heinz ketchup and grab some tomatoes from Kano and mash them up!!! Ok, Dad, I'll let you tell them yourself. I think there'll be a riot in the house once they hear all that!

CHAPTER FOUR:

I Can't Kill Myself Oh!

Femi: Search for the artist Timaya on YouTube and you'll discover one of the best songs ever to come out of Nigeria. The song "I Can't Kill Myself" is certainly one that speaks the people's language. Some of the comments on the official YouTube channel include:

"The literal meaning of this song is do your best and leave the rest for God. I can't go over to impress people." - H Iwuoha

"This song saved me from depression. True I can't kill myself." - A Shituma

"I am tired of flat tummy goals, I can't kill myself." - P McCarthy

There are so many more like the above. Have a read of the comments when you have a few moments to spare for laughter. There are some really funny ones! In all the jest, you will perceive a depth of pain expressed in that humour, though. You'll notice a state of mind that says, 'I'll give it all I've got, but at the end of the day, I can't kill myself!' In other words, 'Somethings are just out of my control'. The phrase basically summarises the life philosophy of the average Nigerian which says 'regardless of what happens life goes on and I must be part of the living' in other words, there is always another day. This attitude or belief is why Nigerians often refer to themselves as the happiest people on earth.

You might be surprised to hear this phrase isn't new. It's not a recent slogan construed by the millennials. In fact, I think I have been hearing this for the last 20 or 30 years, maybe not verbatim, but I am certain we've been trying to convey the same message. The message I deduced from the saying was rather different, though. Maybe my rose-tinted glasses made me hear and see it differently, or maybe it was just maturity that made me see/hear a different message. What I heard whenever this phrase was uttered was more along the lines of 'I don't really care so much about this situation, this country, this job, so I am only going to do the minimum. All these issues in society aren't really my concern.'

Contrast that with what we often see in Hollywood movies; a young American ranger goes into a hostage situation, saves his countrymen, and of course there's a beautiful blonde as well for good measure. That stereotype was reiterated so many times in movies that you'll forgive me for thinking, as a young kid, Americans were the best people in the world, and their soldiers would lay their lives down for their country at the drop of a hat.

Now, compare that with the scenes most of us in Africa grew up with; corrupt government officials, corrupt security personnel, and the average man on the street seeming powerless to effect any meaningful change. So, I often told myself, and I am sure many of you did the same, this situation was never going to change. It's always been this way and will always be this way, so either join the club or make your way to another country. Put another way, 'We can't kill ourselves'.

The ordinary citizen, though tired of corruption and marginalization, could not be bothered to do anything about it. This certainly didn't make me feel proud of my country and fellow men. We can't kill ourselves! How about the marines and the Israelis? How about the South Africans who marched and fought until independence? I would ponder these questions. And so, for many years, I was sold to that notion, that Nigerians, and indeed most Africans, think 'I can't kill myself'. All this as the backdrop to my attending a secondary school where we hoisted the Nigerian flag on a daily basis, sang the anthem and pledged our allegiance to the nation, just didn't add up.

I was, therefore, very glad, grinning from ear to ear, when I first heard about the demonstrations in Nigeria, symbolised by the Lekki toll gate. At last, some patriotic Nigerians; some Nigerians 'who can kill themselves'. Some young folks who could live up to the expectation of those Hollywood American heroes; some Nigerians actually willing to stand up for the truth and fight for their human rights and dignity. Wow! These guys were like heroes to me, and I am sure most of us watching our flat screens from the comfort of our homes felt the same way.

In the midst of the demonstrations and fight for justice, I think we were all reminded that there was once a generation of Nigerians who did fight for their rights and freedom, though we might not speak about it much. There was once a civil war in Nigeria. History might label it as an ethnic war, but origins of the conflict were certainly not just down to ethnicity. So, my quest in this chapter is to pick my old man's brains about this period of our history and try to figure out what drove those people to say 'I can kill myself'.

In 2019, I read a book titled *Half of a Yellow Sun*. What an absolutely fabulous read! Entertaining, enlightening, engaging and well written, and, most of all, educative for me. Though fictional, it taught me more about the Biafra war than I had learned at Navy Secondary School. It created an appetite in me to go and learn more about the history of that time. I also found something really interesting after randomly polling several of my friends and old classmates. No one seemed to know much about this era. Most of us couldn't even remember when the war was fought, even less of the devastation it caused.

In our defence, I guess since we weren't born or weren't old enough at the time, it didn't come naturally to us to read up and engage in conversations that would take us back in history. I know you are thinking, 'Femi! What a lame excuse!' I honestly couldn't think of a better one for my generation. Maybe it's something more sinister, like the nation avoiding talking about that part of history due to fear of tensions flaring up or fear or persecution.

Here, in the UK, we skim over the history of the slave trade, or even make it like an American issue. Abolition was a British strategy, we often insinuate. I sense that sort of vibe here as well, Dad. The first time I asked you about this topic, I recall you mentioned that it was ancient history; that no one wanted to hear about it. That's ironic, because 100 years later, people still want to know what happened during the world wars. Switch on the *Discovery* channel, and within a couple of hours, there's bound to be a documentary about World War 1 or 2. In fact, having watched so many of those documentaries, I find myself able to discuss some of the military and political strategies deployed in the wars, and those are wars that had little or nothing to do with African history, although many Africans did fight in those wars.

I am aware this part of history might be sensitive for you and people of your generation, so I'll be cognisant of that in our discussions. So, tell us a story, Dad. What was it like being a young man at this time? Was it like what you see in the movies? Country goes to war; young patriotic men sign up to defend the cause. Did you have an option to join the forces?

Dad: Let me start by giving you and our readers a brief history of the conflict. I assume most readers might not be aware of the history of that period. The Nigerian army of the early 1960s had a number of well-educated and well-trained officers, just as you had people like myself well trained in agriculture. They were young men in their mid-20s to early 30s. They had been exposed to the military leaders of the West, and had the best military training of the time. These young men had been exposed to ideals of nationhood and building a people. They had ideas as to how a nation should be governed, and there's no doubt that they were nationalistic and meant well for the nation of Nigeria, which was then only five years old as an independent nation. These young military officers had been exposed to the birth of a nation, and many of them felt a sense of duty to protect our baby nation.

At the time, Nigeria was being governed under a federal constitution, in which three regional governments operated and were coordinated by a federal or central government. The politicians, in the views of a few young officers, were not governing well. They were adjudged to be corrupt and feudalistic. The young officers also felt that the Northern Region had an undue advantage over the other two regions, by reason of their higher population. This is a challenge we are still grappling with today, and it dates back to when Nigeria was formed in 1914.

They then staged a coup d'etat, sacked both the federal and regional governments and set up a unitary government, then installed their superior officers to govern the nation. Unfortunately, their plan to kill some top political figures throughout the country was badly carried out. They killed some leaders in the North and the West, and some senior military officers from these regions, and spared the lives of Eastern leaders. The leaders of the coup planners were Ibo officers, but some Yoruba officers also joined them.

They handed over the government to the most senior officer, who happened to be an Ibo man. The Northern leaders were seriously aggrieved and felt humiliated, and this led to a counter coup six months later. This time, it was led by Northern military officers, and many Ibo people all over the country were under threat of being killed, so they started a mass migration to the East. Many Ibo officers and civilians were killed all over the country as reprisal for their action.

Lieutenant Colonel Odumeguru Ojukwu was the most senior surviving Ibo officer, and he led the Eastern region to break away from Nigeria and form a new nation, which they named Biafra. Efforts to mediate between the warring parties by some African nations failed. The Government of Nigeria, under the new military administration, headed by Lieutenant Colonel Yakubu Gowon, decided to keep Nigeria as one united entity and proceeded to take military action to quash the rebellion.

What started as a small-scale military action soon became a full-scale civil war, which lasted from 1967 to 1970. Millions of people died in the war, including soldiers and civilians from all sides, but mostly Easterners. The superior military force of Nigeria subdued Biafra, and they surrendered formally in January 1970. Reconciliation and reconstruction of damaged infrastructure started a few months after the war ended.

The war might have been averted if some Western countries, who were interested in exploiting the oil resources in the East, had not sided with the East. They encouraged the leaders in the East to believe that they were no longer safe in Nigeria because of the killing of many Ibos in the North, and to secede.

Femi: Thanks for that whistle-stop tour, Dad. Did you feel pressure to condemn the war or atrocities? How did you relate to your Ibo friends or colleagues, if you had any at the time? And the same for the Hausa ones? How did the war/war time shape your thinking and affect you?

Dad: The civil war was fought largely by the conventional armed forces personnel. It was not necessary to have mass mobilization of the citizens. They only stepped up recruitment of able and willing people. Furthermore, I was already a senior civil servant, actively promoting food production to ensure adequate food supply in the country, so enlisting didn't cross my mind. That wasn't the case for many young Ibo professionals of my age at the time, though. As the fighting intensified, so did the need for many more Ibo men to be conscripted.

The theatre of war was mainly in the Eastern Region, so

the exposure of the rest of the country to real military action was minimal. However, the atmosphere was generally tense. Considering the government of the day was a military one, dissent and demonstrations against the war weren't encouraged. On one occasion, a Biafran aircraft dropped a bomb in the Yaba area of Lagos, on a cinema house. Thereafter, all streetlights were permanently switched off to make it difficult for aircrafts to locate strategic installations, such as the broadcasting house, power generating stations, etc. Even the *Owambe* parties that Lagos was known for had to stop for some time. The brunt of the war was borne by the Eastern civilian population. There was significant loss of life in towns and villages located in the path of fighting. The effect of the war was particularly bad for the women and children, as millions starved due to the economic blockade imposed on the Biafrans by the Nigerian military.

The post-war effect lingered for many years. Many Ibos were still able to recover the properties they had abandoned at the peak of the crisis in the South years after the war. The loss of position in the federal public service, the military and public corporations made Ibos remain bitter many years after the war, in spite of Government efforts at reconciliation and reconstruction. This has recently fuelled a renewed agitation for the actualization of the Biafra dream.

Till this day, there is still a feeling of marginalization by many Ibos.

Fortunately, the Ibos have regained commanding heights in commerce and industry due to their spirit of enterprise.

Femi: As I have come to realise, there were so many forces at play at that time, from the French who initially supported the Biafrans to the African nations who voiced their allegiance to countries as far away as Haiti. The conflict seems to have had a much more global perspective than I imagined. I always thought it was just a bunch of locals disagreeing over resources.

The obvious cultural and religious differences that, to this day, still threaten the union of the Nigerian Republic also played a significant role in shaping the conflict, so I wonder, how did the aftermath of the conflict shape some of the agricultural policies you spent so many years implementing? Was there concern about the Government investing/developing farming in the Eastern states, for example?

Dad: It is important to know that, before the civil war, there was harmony among the many tribes and ethnic groupings. There was also religious tolerance all over the country. Southerners and Northerners lived peacefully together. I am not saying it was a perfect system, but it certainly didn't feel like there was disharmony amongst the various tribes.

The division started to emerge when politicians seeking power began to play one tribe against the other, invoking religious sentiments to gain popularity. Some mischievous Western interests exaggerated our divisions by expounding the theory of the North being predominantly Muslim versus the South being predominantly Christian. Recently, the situation is being compounded by religious extremists, particularly Boko Haram and ISWAP, who pretend to be spreading Islam by force. Some other people, who can be called criminal gangs, have since joined in the confusion by raiding communities and schools, kidnapping, looting, and burning down villages. Others specialise in cattle rustling. The whole thing is taking a sub-regional dimension as herdsmen from the West African sub-region are entering Nigeria to destabilise the farming systems. This is proving challenging for the Government to contain, even though security has been significantly stepped up in the affected regions.

I am not going to be drawn into the debate of whether Nigeria should remain as one nation. Rather, I would like to end this chapter with a quote from Chinua Achebe: "The only thing we have learnt from experience is that we learn nothing from experience." That said, the obvious solution to unity is to ensure power is devolved to the states, so they can be resourceful and accountable for their economic and social development.

CHAPTER FIVE:

Tribal Marks

Femi: Our visit to Nigeria in 2014 was such a memorable one. It was the first time for my then six-year-old daughter. It was an unforgettable holiday. For her, it was the first time being in a place with so many people that look just like she does; the first time seeing so many bad roads; seeing so many colourful houses; seeing people hawking in the streets; the first time being in some of the biggest houses she'd ever seen. It was certainly a first in many respects.

Amongst the many firsts was also her first time seeing people with unusual marks on their faces. "Why does that lady's face look like that?" "How?" I said. "Like that, Dad, you know, hmm?" I guess that's how I must have felt the first time I noticed someone with a tribal mark.

As a young boy growing up in Lagos, it wasn't too common, but certainly common enough to notice a few people at the market, or whenever we went to our hometown in Ilé-Ifẹ̀. For me, though, it became all too familiar. I can still remember one of the drivers who took me to school had tribal marks, so I got to see it daily for a few years. I guess that's why I never asked the question, but I certainly never knew the origin. If anything, I ignorantly assumed only the less privileged had the marks on their faces, but this didn't prove so true as I grew older and made friends who had marks in school. In fact, the prettiest girl I know has a mark on her face. A former president of Nigeria is awash with marks on his face, so it is nothing to do with status, class or level of education.

For my daughter, this was completely alien though, and I guess she isn't the only one in this boat. There must be millions of kids, and indeed adults (myself being one), who have wondered, 'Why is that person's face like that?' Or 'Who did that to you?' 'How could your parents be so mean?!' 'This is child abuse!' (Check out a few pictures on Google, and you will see what I mean). 'If my parents had done that to me, I would never have spoken to them again!' Those are probably a few of the thoughts that go through the minds of children as they see the marked faces, or shall I say, those are the thoughts that have gone through my mind, but I am sure I am not alone here.

While writing this chapter, I discovered that tribal marks are not peculiar to the Yoruba folks in Nigeria. In fact, in Papua New Guinea, for example, the young men have their backs, shoulders and torsos marked in the shape of crocodiles, as part of an initiation ceremony into adulthood, so there is no escaping it for some of the young men in certain tribes.

So, over to you, Dad. Was this common place in your time? How did you escape your face being marked? Your dad was a chief after all, so I would have thought this would have been standard for you.

Dad: *(laughing)* I didn't escape, as you put it. Tribal marks, known as '*Ila*' in Yoruba language, were actually a thing of beauty!

Femi: Beauty! Did I hear you right, Dad?! Why would you cut someone's face to beautify them?

Dad: From Egypt to Sudan to Kenya, you will find well-documented examples of the different cultures using tribal marks to denote beauty. Marks on the face and other parts of the body were ways people, especially young ladies, enhanced their beauty. You must remember, before the world was colonised, before globalization, beauty was certainly more reflective of our localities, and cultures. It was what we knew. If you never saw a Hollywood blonde on your screen being presented as the ideal of beauty all the time, you might not automatically associate beauty with a blonde lady. That's not to say blonde ladies aren't beautiful.

Femi: Dad, now this is getting weird. You and I sitting and talking about blondes just does not sound right. Can we get back to why people's faces were marked please?

Dad: In the days of old, and even up till recently, marks on the face were seen just as the tattoos you see on the sports stars and music artists. These tribal marks are just more painful and irreversible compared to tattoos. *Ila*, as it's known in Yoruba language, is also known to have been used as a way of identification. Names in the Yoruba culture were and still are a very important source of identifying clan members. Much of the tribe would have lived in clans. The clans offered protection and agricultural opportunities, which was the primary source of subsistence; therefore, knowing which clan you belonged to was a matter of life and death at times. As a result, parents took *ila* as their responsibility. During the slave trade era, when most tribal groups were often raided by warriors from foreign lands, people were often displaced, captured and enslaved. Therefore, people needed a way to easily identify one another. This was even more important for children. You can imagine that an adult would be unlikely to forget his name or his language, even after many years of capture, but children taken at a tender age would lose their sense of identity in no time. The tribal marks ensured there was always a way to be identified if the children returned home or were found. So, you see, many cultures proudly wore and still wear their marks as a symbol of who they are and what they represent.

Recently, I heard the story of a young woman of a Yoruba father and an Ibo mother, with very distinct facial marks, who appeared on social media asking for help to locate her father. She had been taken to Ibo land as a little child, and the mother had broken ties with her father, who was now deceased. She spoke perfect Ibo but not a word of Yoruba and decided to go searching for her relatives when she was older. Fortunately, an Ibadan chief, who identified the marks, helped her locate her people by using her facial marks as a clue. So, you see, even in the digital age, some traditions still have some value to add.

Femi: Now you put it that way, I see why it would have been quite important to identify each other very quickly, especially in times of danger. Are there other reasons people had *ila*?

Dad: Oh yes! Apart from beauty and cultural identification, another form of body marks are small insertions on the face, chest, wrists or other parts of the body. This is called *'gbere'*. An insertion is made on the body, and then some native medicine is rubbed into the cut, so this enters the blood stream. This is meant to drive away evil spirits, demonic attacks and even common ailments such as migraine. You can imagine that mortality rates amongst children was quite high compared to current times. This was a particular challenge when I was growing up, but I'll talk more about that in another chapter. So, therefore, parents of yester years would have resorted to whatever means necessary to protect children from serious illness and death. This particular reason is the reason I believe the practice persisted long after the other reasons. Our society is one where a lot of people practice, or shall I say used to practice, two religions, and therefore, they would take elements from each religion, Christianity, Islam and traditional religions, such as Ifa and Ogun, and combine these with cultural practices passed down from previous generations. Though marking children anywhere on their body is now officially banned in some states in Nigeria, I suspect the populace in the heart of the rural areas still continue the practice and are likely to keep doing so for some time to come. Some parents in traditional settings still put face marks on the eldest son or daughter as a memorial so that the family identify will not be lost, while the other children of the family are left unmarked.

Femi: So, Dad, did you ever witness another child being given *ila* or *gbere* when you were younger? And, if yes, how did you feel, or was it a ceremony hidden from the glare of family members and friends?

Dad: I have personally seen it done on several occasions. You should note that giving people facial identification marks and *gbere* for protection was done within each household but not in secret. Other children sometimes watched while it was being done. The procedure was carried out by specially trained traditional people, using a scalpel or needle. It was only mildly painful when done by skilled people. They would usually apply some disinfectant powder, which allowed it to heal quickly without festering and with marks easily readable. I suppose it might look unpleasant for you, especially when you see the pictures on the internet, but for us who grew up around this, it was normal.

The next time you see someone with a mark on their face or their body, remember, it could be a thing of beauty. You can go ahead and ask them what the mark represents in the same way you admire and ask about tattoos. You'll be pleasantly surprised; they'll gladly respond to you.

CHAPTER SIX:

Coming to America

Femi: It's 20:00hrs BST on a certain day, August 1986. I can't quite recall the exact date. I am sitting in the window seat of a DC 10, waiting for the tow vehicle to drag the aircraft so it can dock with the jet bridge. A few passengers have already unfastened their belts in a bid to make an early exit. I am in no hurry to get off the plane though. Rather, I am fascinated as I repeatedly look at my watch and look out the window. The sun is bright and high up in the sky, like its 4pm in the afternoon. It was quite surreal!

That was my first experience of a European summer. Seeing the sun still shining till 9pm was a novelty that still lingers 30 years on. As a kid, I guess I was thinking, 'Wow! Mum doesn't have to tell me to come into the house by 6:30pm,' which is the usual time for sunset in Lagos.

As I reminisce about that first trip to Europe, I can't help but think about your experience of travel to the Western world for the first time 22 years earlier. It must have been more of a shock than mine. At least

I had been on an aeroplane before my first foreign travel, watched colour TV for many years, and had an idea what England looked like from reading Famous Five, though London didn't match the description I had envisioned.

For you, though, what was it like leaving Ilé-Ifẹ̀ for Wisconsin? How did you adjust? How did anyone understand your accent? It would have sounded so fresh, as your grandchildren would say! Were you scared of boarding a plane? I can just picture you coming out of the plane, or was it a boat in 1964? (lol) As you arrived in Wisconsin, did you have funny African clothes on? Was your accent so thick that the air hostesses could not understand you? Did anyone call you Kunta Kinte? Or was it more like the scene in *Coming to America,* when Prince Akeem and Simi walk into the airport with fur and other African ornaments all over them? The prince tries to blend in, but it is too obvious he isn't from those parts. Your father was a wealthy chief, so did you arrive in the US of A in proper *African* style?

By the way, these are serious questions, Dad. I am genuinely unaware of what it must have been like leaving a village in Africa in the 1960s and heading for the United States.

Dad: (laughs) My arrival in the USA was not comical like you have described in the movie; far from it. Though, I must admit, I am yet to see the movie, but I doubt it was anything like my arrival in the USA.

In those days, travelling abroad to study was for a few privileged people whose parents had the means or won a government scholarship. I studied up till university level in Nigeria, and, fortunately for me, the United States Agency for International Developments started an intergovernmental training programme in the early 1960s. As a civil servant in the Western Region of Nigeria, I was selected to study animal science at post-graduate level at the University of Wisconsin, Madison, USA.

While there was still plenty of sea travel in those days, air travel had become more accessible, and so I travelled by air. I left Ikeja Lagos Airport on a British Overseas Airways Corporation (BOAC) aircraft to London on January 4th, 1964. BOAC later merged with British Caledonian; I can't remember the exact time it became British Airways. I travelled in the company of a few other colleagues in the service of the then Western Region of Nigeria. We arrived in London at about 6.00am on January 5th, then transhipped onto a Pan American Airways direct to Washington DC Dulles Airport.

Although we were well equipped with winter clothing and a topcoat, landing in mid-winter for the first time, in snow and freezing temperatures, was not fun at all, but it was a mixture of curiosity, excitement and discomfort. After about 10 days orientation with students from several developing countries, we were all dispatched to various universities in the Midwest. I went to Madison, Wisconsin, and, to my surprise, it was much colder than Washington DC. I recall myself staggering in knee-deep snow, dripping at the nose, with numb fingers and toes, in my first few days of orientation on campus, but I soon adjusted and settled down to my programme in the Department of Dairy Science. Settling down was very smooth because Americans were very warm and friendly to foreign students. And, within a few weeks, I fell in love with coffee, like most Americans. I had a wonderful time while schooling in America. My colonial teachers in my younger days gave me a sound education, and the American schooling system and society taught me how to dream and aspire to do great things. My one take-away from America in the 1960s was 'anything is possible'.

CHAPTER SEVEN:

Egunje

Femi: It must have been around 1984/85. I was in primary school at this time, and I recall a man coming to the house and showing you a Mercedes, much like a salesman would when trying to sell you a car. In fact, I recall the car was white with a black interior. Even at that age, I knew the car was different. I vividly remember the famous Mercedes breakdown triangle hanging off the boot as the man opened the boot to show off the features of the car. At the time, I probably thought it was one of your official cars, so I was excited. I mean, who wouldn't want to be taken to school in a Mercedes. 'Ditch the Peugeot 504,' I must have thought.

I cannot quite recollect how I got to find out the story of that car. Maybe I overheard conversations or just put two and two together but as I grew older, I realized what had taken place. A government contractor, who was also your friend, offered you a brand-new, white Mercedes Benz, brought it to the house, and then you rejected the car. The reaction from my teenage friends when I recounted this story was priceless. One or two of them might have even asked if you are a true Nigerian.

Yet that's not the only demonstration of integrity and honesty I recall you displayed in front of me as a child. To every parent out there, it is true; children are like tape recorders. They are watching your every move. I recall another example. This time I received several phone calls on your behalf (on the home phone; no mobile phones then!) from a certain gentleman who had been chasing after you for a while. I suspect he had tried to reach you in the office, and then found his way to the house eventually. I was a bit older by this time, so I could guess the score. He was an importer, though I'm not sure what he wanted to import, I suspect items that were on the plant quarantine or import ban list. He offered you a bribe so he could import his goods, and you got quite upset. You were both sitting in the guest reception room, and suddenly, you stood up and walked the man out of the house and shouted for him never to return.

As a young teen, I was thinking, '*Kai kai kai*! This man doesn't want to collect *egunje*' (translated 'Boy! Oh boy! He doesn't want to collect a bribe,' for my non-Nigerian readers). If only I had been the one who had opened the front door, I would have at least got something in my pocket before you sent him packing!

Do you remember those events, Dad? And, more importantly, this is a question I have been waiting to ask all my life! How could you turn down that white Mercedes Benz!!! I would have been the coolest kid on the block!

Dad: Let me answer that by asking you a question, Femi. Cast your mind back to the mid-1990s, while you were in secondary school. What car was I driving and often picked you up from school with?

Femi: Ok, you got me there, Dad! I get the lesson.

Dad: Exactly, all I had to do was continue working honestly, and in a few years, I could afford to buy the same car. The difference is, I slept like a baby at night knowing I didn't owe the car to anyone.

Femi: One more question, Dad. How much did the guy (importer) offer you?

Dad: Next question, please! All joking aside, the attempts to bribe me were so numerous that it is difficult for me to remember specific cases.

Femi: *(laughing out loud)* Ok, let me ask a question I think you'll answer. How did you stay in a prestigious government job without getting corrupt? I mean, those are two examples I recall. I am sure there were numerous other ones I am not aware of. It's one thing sticking to your principles, but then if everybody around you doesn't follow those principles, how do you swim against the current? How do you survive?

Dad: Son! This is what separates the men from the boys! It's my turn to laugh!

I am not going to pretend like I have all the answers to this question. I can only really talk from my own perspective; the habits, principles, and guardrails I have developed.

I served in the Nigerian Civil Service, both at the federal and state levels, rising to the prestigious position of Federal Director of Agriculture, and never compromised my integrity. And the first answer I want you to take note of is 'I served'.

Even though I headed the department that had by far the largest portion of Federal Government appropriation for agriculture, including the millions of naira for fertilizer importation, it never crossed my mind to compromise my integrity.

Femi: Wow wow wow! Dad, this is even larger than I thought! Did you say millions? So my story of the Mercedes Benz is like chicken change then.

Dad: Yes, that's correct. For many years, successive governments poured millions (billions by the time the naira was devalued) into the agricultural sector in an effort to kickstart the industry. In this period, three factors influenced my stand. First was the family name. We are very proud of the legacy of the good name our father left, and all the first line of children from his 20 plus wives have done our best to maintain the family reputation. In addition to that, we had great mentors, such as Chief S.O. Adebo, Dr TSB Aribisala, etc. Secondly, as a product of Government College Ibadan up to the early 1960s, I was expected to be of exemplary character. Thirdly, you will recall that I have been a committed Christian for several decades. The acquisition of material wealth has never been a major consideration in my life. We thank God it has all played out well, even up to your own generation.

Femi: I understand your faith stance, Dad, yet that isn't a determinant of integrity in the current Nigerian society. And, to an extent, I understand what it means to defend the family name. But your school's name; I don't get that one. How could an institution you attended as a child have such an influence on your character?

Dad: You will be surprised by the results of positive subliminal messages being showered on impressionable children continually for years. I mean, we were constantly reminded: 'You are the future of the nation; the leaders of tomorrow.' At home, that message was reinforced over and over by my father, who constantly modelled hard work and integrity.

That's my foundation and the principles that helped me manage success in middle age. Now, talking of the larger society, Nigeria of 60 or 70 years ago was a highly disciplined society. At the family and local level, the standard of morality was very high. People who stole were easily apprehended and severely punished. Some of such people were so ashamed that they moved out of their normal place of abode to a place where they were unknown. At the national level, a high standard of administration was instituted by the British. Laxity was severely punished, and this served as a deterrent. Following the departure of the British administrators, standards of morality started to fall. Discipline was weakened by ethnic and religious considerations. Public officers who stole money got away with it, and it soon spread to all cadres of staff and office holders. Now, it has become so endemic in the Nigerian society that public officers and politicians amass wealth at the expense of the masses. The recent uprising of the youth of the nation is a reaction to this development, so lasting change to the fallen morality is a very urgent desideratum.

Femi: So, what would you say to the young civil servant of today, whose environment is much worse than the one you grew up in? How would he survive without being corrupt?

Dad: Regardless of changing economic circumstances, a good upbringing will always separate the good guy from the rest of the pack. The good news is that, as bad as things seem in Nigeria today, there are still many honest public servants. I was certainly not the only one in my time, just like Elijah wasn't the only undefiled prophet of his time. There will come a time when honesty will be the order of the day, and upright members of society will be promoted and celebrated. And, as their number increases, things will turn around again. The Western countries that normally condemn us today were once like us. Even now, there is still a high level of corruption among them. Never mind the Western media about the corruption in Nigeria; you just have to remember that most of the stolen wealth ends up in Western banks.

CHAPTER EIGHT:

Chief Chief!

Femi: One of Grandma's favourite TV programmes is *The Bisi Olatilo Show*. 'Bisi who?' Some of our readers in the diaspora have probably never heard of the show. If that's you, picture this: The show is like *OK!* magazine but on TV, so when anyone of notable standing in society is having a celebration, the event gets aired on the TV show, provided they have the means to pay for the episode.

Of the four or five events shown on each episode, you'll notice one thing that's synonymous: Chief! Yep, every father of the bride, every man or woman celebrating his or her landmark birthday, usually 50, 60 or 70, is a chief, a chief's wife, a senator, or Alhaji, without exception. It makes me wonder, how many chiefs do we have in Nigeria? Is there a chief per 100 persons in society? Is every rich person in Nigeria a chief? If I wanted to become a chief, what do I have to do?

Dad: In Yoruba land, and Ilé-Ifẹ̀ in particular, chieftaincy is a very important socio-cultural matter. In every community, there is a spiritual and administrative head. He is called '*Oba*' or '*Baale*', depending on the size and age of the community. He is supported by a number of chiefs for the administration of the community, and they maintain law and order. This arrangement was in place before colonial administration, and dates back hundreds maybe thousands of years.

In recent years, chieftaincy has evolved in several dimensions, though the basic structure is still similar to what our forefathers handed down to us. In Ifẹ̀ land the paramount ruler is called the '*Ooni*' and he presides over the geographical expression called Ifẹ̀ division. This has now been split into several local government areas and administrative units, until recently the Ooni had administrative authority over the whole division and was assisted by a group of chiefs who represented the major quarters of the Ilé-Ifẹ̀, namely Iremo, Ilare, Moore, Ilode,Iraye and Okerewe, (Okerewe is where I am from). In addition to the chiefs representing their towns/villages the Ooni also appoints two chiefs by virtue of their distinction in character and wide accomplishments. These eight chiefs constituted the administrative entity with the Ooni at the head known as the 'Ooni in council'. The proclamations and decisions of the council was binding on all Ife citizens.

There is a second group of chiefs known as the 'Modewa' also eight in number their primary function is to serve as administrative staff in the palace, if this was a government organisation you could refer to these chiefs as the civil servants, they were the ones who propagated and enforced the decisions of the council.

Then we have a third class of chiefs, known as the 'Onisoro' their function is to supervise the ceremonies pertaining to the over 201 deities or local gods for which Ifẹ is well known. While the first two classes of chiefs are stipendiary, the Onisoro chief aren't, they are taken care of by the families and clans to which the gods belong to, so they can spend all their time in ceremonial duties.

Femi: Dad!! I can just imagine, when the children read the above paragraph, they will run screaming into my room asking, is grandpa among the idol worshipers?!!! Are the chiefs worshiping deities?

Dad: Laughing! Tell the kids to calm down and keep on reading.

From a Christian perspective, yes, these practices of deity worship is idolatry, but then, these traditions have been in existence long before Christianity landed on the shores of Africa, so the traditionalists do not see it that way. To make it more interesting, a lot of chiefs are also Christians or Muslims. We will talk more about this in later chapters.

Let's get back to how chiefs are selected, using Ilé-Ifẹ̀ as an example. The fourth class of chiefs is a recent development, these are the ones you are more familiar with, they can be called 'honorific' chiefs. They are made chiefs at the pleasure of the *Ooni* and are selected for their distinction in social and philanthropic service to the community. For instance, a doctor or engineer who rendered great service to the community is honoured with a chieftaincy title, similar to when the Queen of England honours a distinguished person from any part of the Commonwealth with an OBE or MBE. The honorific title holders have no part in the administration of the community or in the worship of deities. They don't have to be indigenes of the community, unlike the other title holders. The *Modewas* and *Onisoro* have some remuneration for their services, while the honorific chiefs do not, they are often already wealthy member of the community, so when you watch the Bisi Olatilow show or open a copy of the OK magazine the chief you spot in there is likely to be an honorific chief.

The selection process for chiefs and Obas used to be very lengthy, and the leadership in the community would sift through all aspects of that person's character before they are honoured with a title. In Yoruba land the qualities that were and are still needed include, *làákà'yè* (that is someone of wisdom and understanding, *Ìwà Omolúàbí* (that is someone with integrity), *anísélápá tí kìíse òle* (that is someone with a means of livelihood who can support themselves). You also have *iyi* (which simply means a person of honour). All these qualities and many more I haven't named ensured that each person that was called to serve the *Oba* and his community was adequately equipped for the mandate.

In most Yoruba communities of today, there are what are referred to as 'ruling houses', usually about four or five. *Obas* are selected from ruling houses in rotation, which are agreed and gazetted by the Government. In Benin Kingdom, and most Emirates in Northern Nigeria, *Obaship* is hereditary and shifts from father to son on the demise of the former.

Under the new arrangement of federal, state and local governments, the administration of communities has shifted from traditional rulers to the three tiers of government. State and local government authorities still manage to carve out advisory roles for *Obas* to make them relevant.

Femi: If the role of the chiefs is now largely advisory and bi-partisan, why is it still a coveted position? Why are they celebrated like celebrities, and why does every rich Nigerian, or shall I say a lot of rich Nigerians from the South, have a chieftaincy title?

Dad: Though the chiefs and *Obas* do not hold any judicial, political, or administrative offices on the basis of their titles, they still carry a lot of clout, especially the top *Obas*, such as the *Ooni*. Our politicians still court and woo them, as they can decide political winners and losers. Outside of the big cities, in towns and villages the country over, the local chiefs and *Obas* still preside over small disputes and provide leadership to many of the local communities. Furthermore, the honorific chiefs are often accomplished and wealthy members of the society. Adding the title to the name completes the package so to speak.

We are a nation of title seekers, and a lot of us like to be praised with our titles. You must also remember that the Yoruba language and culture is very clan based, and each clan has what you call '*oriki*'. These are the spoken family heritage or praise songs; something that distinguishes the clan family from others. If you are reading this book and you've never heard your *oriki*, I suggest you ask your parents or grandparents. It's very rich traditional poetry, so I guess there is something in us as a people that likes the praises and titles being showered on us.

Femi: You can say that again, Dad! I recall you had a few friends whose titles were Chief Eng., Chief Doc, Chief, Chief Architect. How come you weren't made a chief, Dad?

Dad: There are several reasons why a notable person in society may not be a chief. Namely, by tradition, a prince from an Ifẹ ruling house does not accept a chieftaincy title; the head of the princes from each ruling house is honoured with a title called 'Sooko'. Therefore, they cannot be chiefs at the same time. Some people will not accept a chieftaincy title on religious grounds, because some of the titles entail rituals, whilst other titles involve some form of cultism.

In the colonial times, civil servants were not allowed to take titles due to conflict of interest. As for me, I didn't take a chieftaincy title for two reasons. First, I was away from home, working as a civil servant, first at state level, and later at the Federal for over 35 years, and even after retirement, I stayed away until a few years ago. Secondly, my involvement in church activities did not permit me. Thirdly, having a chieftaincy title did not appeal to me, because I was already accomplished in many respects. One of these days, you will meet Chief the Hon Dr Lamorin Bobagunwa of Dagbolu (laughs). Nigerians simply love titles!

CHAPTER NINE:

Twenty Twenty

Femi: Most people in the world would rather forget the year 2020. There was more than enough bad news to last a life time, all in the space of 12 months. I recall reading a comment that encapsulated the way a lot of people must have felt at the time: "If the world were a bus, could I get off at the next bus stop? I'll wait for the bus 2020 to go, with all its terrifying news, and then hop on the next bus, with hopes and dreams that the world would have magically healed and I could go back to life as I once knew it."

Despite the longing for amnesia about the year, the killing of a black American man streamed live for the world to see has validated our thoughts about race relations. It has evoked a spirit for justice. It has emboldened people who always wanted to speak to ask questions they had never had the opportunity to ask.

One of the most curious developments that emanated from the horrible event were the historical debates on slavery and colonialism. You would have seen statues being flung into the river or disfigured with graffiti on every news network, and the call from the mainstream media for all symbols of colonialism to be removed from public places. Unsurprisingly, it did not take long before the nationalists emerged with their counter arguments: "We are proud of our heritage," the headlines read. In other words, 'Those who don't like it have a choice of where to live'.

As an immigrant with children who know no other country as theirs, other than the UK, I am glad it didn't escalate beyond the words in the headlines and social media. The cat had been let out of the bag, though, and there were many companies and government organisations who started doing some soul searching. Some made immediate adjustments to policies, while others started initiatives aiming to address the all too obvious divide amongst their white and non-white colleagues at all levels.

One question in particular kept bugging me, though, and I am sure I am not the only one who was asking this question. What was it like during the colonial times? Around about this time, I stumbled upon a documentary, *Journey of an African Colony*, which was absolutely fascinating. So much history! Frankly, that series should be history 101 for anyone wanting to learn about the history of colonialism and who would like to hear it from the victims' perspective.

At this point, I am tempted to ask, Dad, was colonialism a good thing for Nigeria and other African countries? That was one of the discussions trending on social media in 2020. I suspect that question could lead into a never-ending dialogue. There is also the risk that some of the readers have a sharp divide in their opinions. So, rather than ask that, what I would like to know is, what was it like for you as a young man growing up in a country colonised by a foreign power.

Dad: I was born in 1935, over 30 years after the British colonised Nigeria, so by the time I was growing up, the colonialism was already well established in the nation. I didn't experience the initial shock, bewilderment, excitement or embarrassment that my parents would have felt as the nation was being overrun, therefore my perspective can really only be from the late 1940s, when I was a young lad.

The first thing I will say is, for the everyday man at this time, it didn't really make much of a difference. As young boys and girls, we were more preoccupied with getting an education, playing sports, figuring out how to make a brighter future for ourselves, and just living life, just the same way as you do today. That's not to say there was no tension, or riots, or flash points where locals clashed with the colonial government representatives. There certainly was many of those, but at the time, news didn't travel on the internet as it does now, so you only heard of such events days or even weeks after they occurred.

Growing up as a child, we didn't see many of the colonials. It might have been different had I grown up in the city, I suppose. When we did see a white man, it was a big deal. Apart from the obvious difference in skin colour, they looked different in every way. Their hair, nose, clothing; it was like seeing someone from another planet the first few times. As kids, we would all go wild and scream '*Oyinbo*' ('white man' in Yoruba). If they came around us, one of the missionaries for example, they would be mobbed by the local children, all wanting to touch his hands, or his hair, and just wanting to hear him or her speak. At that age, you are innocent, and just accept that these strange pale-skinned people who come from far-away countries are friendly and here to help.

By the time I got into Government College Ibadan as a teenager in 1951, the sight had become all too familiar. Almost all our teachers were Englishmen. Having English teachers had a lot of advantages, including, to name a few, it meant our command of English became sound very quickly. At the time, the English teachers were very disciplined. They took pride in their jobs, so, therefore, our education was first class. The testament to this is that almost all the friends I went to school with became successful in their various fields of endeavour, from agriculture to banking to judiciary. The pupils taught by the colonial teachers had a very good foundation to build upon. I recall, on average, we had to read a book a week, and the teachers would monitor our progress and check our library cards. Fast forward 70 years later, and I still benefit from that habit, reading all sorts of books and now writing as well.

One area that personally touched me was that of health during the colonial era. Up to the mid-1940s, people in Ifẹ town, where I grew up, used traditional medicine to manage their health. This consisted mainly of the use of roots, herbs and other plant materials to prevent or to cure diseases. Most adults lived up to their 60s, but infant mortality was quite high due mainly to diarrhoea, measles and malaria. I recall that, in one year, 12 children died in our family due to diarrhoea and measles. (In case you are wondering, if 12 died, how many were left; I had over 60 siblings, but that story is for another chapter.)

An aspect of the traditional medicine also included the application of supernatural forces (sometimes referred to as 'voodoo' in the Western world) to heal sick people. This is due to the fact that people believed that evil spirits are at work when a person is sick, especially with mental disorders. Even if a woman had prolonged labour, spiritualists were called in to help. It was also widely believed that medicine men could do no harm to people.

In many rural communities, people still believe in the power of medicine men. There is a thin line of distinction between herbalists, who use various parts of plants and other visible materials, and spiritualists. The former is called '*Onisegun*' and the latter '*babalawo*'. *Onisegun* is what we call the modern-day pharmacist.

As more and more hospitals and health centres were built, so the number of infant deaths decreased. Nursing mothers also became more likely to deliver their children safely, and we saw that first-hand with children born in my home in the 50s and 60s. That said, vaccinations for most childhood diseases became prevalent only about 40 years ago. It could have been much worse if things had been left to continue, though.

Tobi: Let's talk about career, Daddy. Was your career choice influenced by the fact that you had a foreign power ruling the nation? Did you see English men in fancy suits and think, 'Yep, I want to be in a suit also'? Or was it more to do with influence from your parents?

Dad: My career choice, and those of many young men and women, was certainly influenced by the colonials, but also by local heroes, as well as the technology, politics and other socio-economic influences of the time. During the late 1920s and early 1930s, the most known public figures were principals (headmasters) of secondary schools, who were mostly graduates of Fourah Bay College, an overseas college of the University of Durham, located in Sierra-Leone.

Tobi: That's interesting! So, there were Africans studying in other African countries as early as the 1930s? That would never have occurred to me.

Dad: Yes, that's correct. The colonial influence across some nations developed faster than others. Outposts were established, and other social infrastructures, such as schools, were quickly created. The early graduates of the initial wave of formal education were also mostly ordained priests. Among them were Rev. I.O. Ransome Kuti, Rev. Lahanmi, Rev. Adeyefa, Rev. Odutola, Rev. Akinyemi, Rev. Omigbodun, and if we go back a little further people like Bishop Ajayi Crowther who is credited with translation of the English Bible to Yoruba. These heroes were very visible in society, and some of them were into the struggle for Nigerians' independence. They influenced many young men and women to take up studies in liberal arts, thus providing graduates to man public administration and teachers for the rapidly expanding secondary education. At that time, most senior positions in the Civil Service were held by expatriate officers, but as more of us were educated, those administrative positions became indigenised.

By the time we got to the 1950s and 1960s, the career of choice shifted to medicine and law. This shift was influenced by the prestige traditionally attached to the two professions and the perception that they were lucrative in comparison to being a graduate teacher. The mentorship of some of the early nationalists also influenced many young men to join the law profession. The mid-1960s' and early 70s' career choices also shifted to the military, when a spate of military coup d'etats in many African countries shot young military officers into the limelight as they seized political power from the ruling class. Before then, parents would not entertain the idea of their wards joining the military as a career. Similarly, music was a no-go area in that period. Parents regarded musicians as lazy louts.

Tobi: Aha! Dad, so I see why every child born in the 1970s or 1980s was told by their parents they had to be a doctor or lawyer.

Dad: At the time, those parents were right. Those jobs were stable and guaranteed a decent income and standard of living. All that soon changed though, when the discovery of oil and its attendant expansion in the infrastructure development began. There arose a high demand for architects, engineers and other professionals in the construction industry, so the career choices also shifted into these areas. Young men could see architects and engineers riding in the latest car models and living affluent lifestyles. Banking and finance also attracted young people when the oil boom led to the establishment of many banks. Gradually, there followed a shift to the creative arts, such as music, theatre arts, etc, and later to sports. Now, in the current generation, the latest field of preference is information technology, as the demand for skilled people in that area grows worldwide.

In my own case, my father wanted me to study liberal arts so I could be a school principal, like Rev. S. A. Adeyefa, who was then Principal of Oduduwa College Ilé-Ifẹ̀, and a very prominent figure in Ifẹ̀ affairs, but I opted for agriculture, because my father was a successful farmer and produce merchant.

Tobi: Very interesting, Dad. I did not realise, even at that time, children didn't always do what their parents wanted. I thought your generation were super obedient. That's also interesting, because he didn't want you to follow in his footsteps and pointed you in another direction. Rather unusual, especially considering he was successful at this endeavour.

Dad: Parent-child relationships have not changed that much. Fathers will always be there to guide and support. Ultimately, the decision is from your heart. I am glad of the influence he had on me, considering that 50 years after his demise, my family are still deriving income from his investments in agriculture. This background also explains why, at 86, I am still an active farmer in my own right and deriving significant income from farming. In fact, my income from farming is more than my pension from the Civil Service.

Another thing that influenced my choice was the proximity of Government College Ibadan, where l was a student at Moore Plantation, where several expatriate graduates of agriculture were research officers and instructors in the School of Agriculture. They wore short knickers and knee-high stockings, and all rode in cars and land rover vehicles. They were held in high regard and moved with their British compatriots, who were our teachers. In those days, you could count Nigerian graduates of agriculture on the fingers of your hand. I was still highly impressionable at this time. Incidentally, 1 was about the first or second university graduate of agriculture of Ifẹ origin.

Going back to my days at Government College Ibadan, it was a model secondary school patterned after the British public school system. There were only about 10 of them in the country, and they were mostly boys' schools and boarding schools. Many of our teachers were not only British, but they also had military backgrounds coupled with experience of teaching in British public schools. Remember, this was only a few years after World War 2.

Femi: Ahah! Military teachers! No wonder, Dad, it all makes sense now! Your discipline, some of your habits; no wonder, lots of things make sense now! This is probably one of the most revealing facts I have learned from our interviews.

Dad: The result of having such teachers was not only a high standard of academic performance but training in basic practical skills, such as carpentry, metal works, clay modelling, music, theatre arts and sporting activities. It was there I learned to swim, play cricket, hockey and soccer, and even hobbies such as photography were encouraged. We literally had an all-round education. We were encouraged to study engineering, medicine, agriculture and other science-related disciplines. Very few went into liberal arts, law and other humanities-related disciplines.

Going back to the original question of this chapter: what was life like being under colonial rule? I would say life was normal, because that's what I knew at that age. Life was exciting. There was a lot of development going on, lots of new technology. The country was also growing socially and politically as we moved towards being an independent nation. Had I been born 50 years earlier, my outlook might have been different. I wasn't forced to start paying taxes to a king I'd never heard of, nor was I conscripted to go into World War 2 to fight for freedom, even though we were being held hostage in our own land. Like most aspects of life, there are always two sides to the story. Without colonisation, I probably would never have had the opportunity to study agriculture at one of the best universities in the world, but without independence I would never have become Head of Agriculture in the nation, as all senior positions were held by the British. Put another way, make the best of whatever situation you are in. Even in the valley, you can take advantage of the situation, so by the time you get to the higher ground, you'll be ready to rule.

CHAPTER TEN:

Merry Christmas & Barka de Sallah

Femi: Some of my most favourite memories growing up were around the festivals. I remember having live turkeys in the backyard. I must admit, I used to be afraid of those. Rams in the house were the norm during Christmas. Sometimes, we had two rams, so my friends and I would try to make them fight. I enjoyed feeding the animals hay, but I sure didn't like cleaning up after them. As a child, it's one of the things that made Christmas awesome.

Within a few months, Ramadan would be around the corner, and we would be at it again. My late friend Sope and I would sometimes even grab a goat and try to ride it while holding its horns. Even as I write this, I am overwhelmed by the acute nostalgia of those days. I have tried to explain this period to my children, but they just cannot get it. They wonder how we could play with an animal one day, and the next day we would all happily eat the same animal. As for me, these conversations leave me wondering what these festivals were like in your time, Dad. Were they filled with the same festivities, or did you celebrate the traditional festivals more than the religious ones? I assume there were some traditional festivals? And, considering Christianity and Islam are foreign to Africa, how did this all blend in your time.

Dad: Of course, there were loads of native festivals before your time. In most of Yoruba land, various festivals are observed throughout the year. Some of them are religious festivals celebrated in remembrance of ancestral deities, such as Ogun, Sango, Obatala, etc. Others are related to seasons of the year, such as the beginning of the planting and harvest seasons. With the advent of some world religions, such as Christianity and Islam, the observance of traditional religions has been downplayed, though there are prominent ones that continue till this day, such as the Olojo, Edi, Ojude Oba festivals, which are still celebrated with pomp and pageantry.

I was exposed to a lot of the traditional festivals growing up. They were very colourful. It was usually a community affair. The ladies dressed in the same attire, or the men sang certain songs, and the children would be filled with excitement. Sometimes, there were strict rules and curfews associated with the festivals, so it did get unnerving at times as a child, especially when we were forbidden to go outside during the ritual ceremonies. Some of the traditions were more interesting. For example, in some southern communities, you are not supposed to start eating yams in your home until the yam harvest festival has been performed. This involves some rituals, which we can consider as prayers, by the natural ruler or a local native priest in the community. After the ceremony, farmers may begin to sell yams in the village market.

Most of my family were Christians, and my father was a great advocate of the local church, so Christmas and Easter were the big festivals we observed at home. Coming from a very large family made this a lot of fun and gave us wonderful memories. In fact, I think we had more exciting Christmas celebrations during my time of growing up.

Femi: How is that possible, Dad, hmm? You did not have a lot of money. And I do not think your houses would have been that comfortable.

Dad: Irrespective of the economic and social circumstances of our time, our Christmas season was marked by a lot of festivities. In the 1950s, new clothes were made especially for the younger folks. We had really colourful carnivals on the streets, so you could have the whole neighbourhood having a party. Many people fixed marriages, funerals and chieftaincy celebrations for the month of December. Most farmers returned

101

home for several weeks, as December coincides with the harvest period for some food and cash crops, so there was always so much to eat and so much to drink. The whole month was dedicated to celebration, or as you say nowadays, enjoyment! Christmas and New Year's Eve were marked by displays of fireworks. Christians were very particular about attending watch night services on both nights.

Femi: Oh wow, Dad, a whole month of partying in the neighbourhood! I suppose some things haven't changed. Lots of weddings are still fixed for December, and there are still lots of celebrations in our generation. I suppose your small communities made it more intimate, so you probably could attend most of the parties in your neighbourhood.

Dad: That's correct, it was certainly more intimate, and generally there was plenty of money to spend. A lot of eating and drinking took place, though jollof rice wasn't the main party dish at the time. Rice was still only produced in small quantities in Nigeria at that time; hence, it was highly preferred and eaten by the affluent members of the community. Pounded yam was the dominant festive food.

Femi: Dad! Dad! Dad! That statement about rice is going to cause some controversy on the internet! Are you telling me jollof rice is a recent dish in Nigeria? There I was thinking, we as a nation have been eating jollof for hundreds of years in Nigeria.

Dad: Rest assured, it's the same across other countries, so if anyone from Ghana says they've been eating jollof in Ghana for centuries, then they have their history all wrong. So, let's get back to religious festivals. Easter time was also observed, but it was less flamboyant and of a shorter duration, just as you have now, though we still celebrated with parades and picnics.

Similarly, two festivals were observed by Muslims, namely the end of the Ramadan fast and the remembrance of Prophet Ibrahim's sacrifice of his son for the redemption of the people, called Eid Fitri. Both were very colourful occasions with a lot of social interaction, but the latter occasion was marked by the slaughtering of rams by all those who could afford them, and sharing among people of all religions. In the North, they staged Dubar, in which lavishly decorated horses were ridden in the Dubar parade.

In recent years, the celebration of both Christian and Muslim festivals has been moderated by the decline in the economic fortunes of the vast majority. For instance, the making of new clothes and the consumption of a lot of turkeys, chickens and meat have been greatly reduced compared to my time of growing up. Although, the population growth since then has also been exponential, so naturally, it cannot be viable to continue this through the generations.

Femi: So, looking back over the last 70 years, how has religion shaped you? How has it shaped the nation, apart from the festivities?

Dad: Virtually all ethnic or tribal entities in Africa believed in a supreme being who controls the affairs of humans. Most tribes and cultures believed they could not have direct access to the supreme being, and therefore invented their own gods or deities, and used such deities to seek the face of God. In some African cultures, a living object, such as a snake, tree, water, or animal, or non-living, such as a river, mountain or stone, etc, were selected, and sacrifices were offered to the deity at particular times periodically. Prayers were said for the preservation and protection of the ethnic group, and for fertility, so that the tribe would continue to flourish. Prayers were offered at the beginning of the cropping season to ensure a bumper harvest. Similarly, thanksgiving prayers were said at harvest time, though on a much smaller scale. This tradition still continues to this day in many villages across the country, and most will have been diluted with some modern or Western practices as these villages become more exposed.

Let's take a step back before looking at the present impact of religion in my lifetime. Islam was introduced in the 17th century by Fulani people to the northern Nigerian states, whilst Christian missionaries arrived on the southern shores between 1840 and 1845, and both religions spread throughout the country, earlier attempts at introducing Christianity in the 15th and 16th century failed. At present, there is hardly any community in Nigeria that has not been penetrated by either of these religions. One peculiarity of Nigeria in regard to religion is the peaceful co-existence of adherents of the two religions.

Femi: You are so right, Dad! As a kid, having both Muslim and Christian friends was the norm. In fact, I went to the mosque out of curiosity a few times, and my Muslim friends did likewise. I cannot imagine the kids of this generation having that experience.

Dad: That was my experience also. In fact, interfaith marriages were more common a few decades ago due to this tolerance. That was the situation up until about two decades ago, when politicians started to play the card of religion to enlist membership for their political parties. The Yorubas are particularly tolerant in religious matters, such that within the same family, members adopt whichever faith they prefer, and they continue to relate together harmoniously. This is not so in the predominantly Muslim communities in the North.

A small number of people in the middle belt and the South are still adherent to traditional religions, and they operate without let or hindrance, as provided for in the Nigerian constitution.

In recent years, both Christian and Muslim organisations have factionalized into so many denominations and sects. Some Christian bodies have a very large following and very large congregations in big cities but are very thin in rural areas. But the growth of religious organisations of both faiths has not resulted in higher commitment to their tenet. Crime, immorality, and general indiscipline are still on the increase.

It is important to state that the southern parts of the country have a much higher number of people exposed to Western education, due primarily to the activities of Christian missionaries. Hence, the level of literacy, as well as training in the professions, including engineering, law, medicine, etc, is much higher in the South, while the northern populace are predominantly farmers and nomads. With better cooperation and selfless leadership, that difference in religion and livelihood should be at a great advantage to the nation. The North feeds the nation and drives crop exports, while the South industrializes and drives the technological advancement needed to compete on a global stage in this century. My prayer is that your generation and the next will be able to reverse the current trend and change the North versus South narrative and the Muslim versus Christian narrative. Rather, I hope you will be able to solve some of the problems my generation were unable to: educate the North more; focus more on cooperation and lifting the North out of poverty; while at the same time, opening up a new inter-Nigeria economy between the North, South and other parts of the nation. That really is the answer to lifting the nation out of poverty. To do this, though, we must first get back to the time of Merry Christmas & Barka de Sallah.

Epilogue

The theme of this book is getting to know your country, Nigeria, and getting involved in its development to become a first-class global community. You don't have to be physically present to be involved. When you cultivate love for Nigeria, ways to be involved in its development will start to emerge. Over 20 million Nigerians are in the diaspora, so the potential is phenomenal.

Your first step is to expand your knowledge of Nigeria, its people, economy, social-cultural matters and the potential for growth and development. This is why, as an introduction to this book, we have a short chapter titled Civic 101. You may already know much of this information, but a revision is often beneficial. Every Nigerian, at home and abroad, should travel to some part of the country from time to time. This is the easiest way to get to know the country. Some foreigners know the country better than we do.

The book has attempted to look back 60 or 70 years into various facets of social and economic development and has traced our path of development in the field of education, agriculture, industry infrastructure and social development. We have pointed out some failures in our national development and have suggested ways to get back on track and move forward. We have tried in a small way to interest our readers in cultural religious issues with a view to encouraging them to dig deeper. We also encourage Nigerians in the diaspora to deliberately develop a stronger linkage with their ancestral roots. Who knows, it may even result in reverse migration back home as things get better.

About the Author

Mr Oladosu Awoyemi is the author of Growing Old Gracefully, he is an 86-year-old grandfather of 11 grandchildren, a former director of the federal ministry of agriculture in Nigeria. Born in the mid 1930's and having lived through the colonial times, independence, oil boom and many more landmark historical events, he brings a personal perspective to living in Nigeria for the last 7 decades.

Printed in Great Britain
by Amazon